To: ....

From: ....

Published by Barbour Publishing, Inc., P.O. Box 719, Uhrichsville, Ohio 44683, www.barbourbooks.com

Our mission is to publish and distribute inspirational products offering exceptional value and biblical encouragement to the masses.

Printed in China.

Heavenly Humor

BARBOUR
PUBLISHING

A happy heart makes the face cheerful.

PROVERBS 15:13 NIV

Life can be wildly tragic at times,
and I've had my share.
But whatever happens to you,
you have to keep a slightly comic
attitude. In the final analysis,
you have to not forget to laugh.

KATHARINE HEPBURN

Church bulletin bloopers:

Bertha Belch, a missionary from Africa, will speak tonight at Calvary Memorial Church in Racine. Come tonight and hear Bertha Belch all the way from Africa.

The ladies of the church have cast off clothing of every kind, and they may be seen in the church basement on Friday afternoon.

Sunday School Teacher: "Who lived in the Garden of Eden?"

Danny: "The Adams."

Why didn't they play cards on Noah's ark?

Because Noah sat on the deck.

Sunday School Teacher: "Why did Moses wander in the desert for forty years?"

Ginny: "Because he was too stubborn to stop and ask for directions?"

At the height of laughter,
the universe is flung into a
kaleidoscope of new possibilities.

JEAN HOUSTON

What do you call a lemon-eating cat?

A sourpuss.

What do you get from a pampered cow?

Spoiled milk.

What composer is the favorite among dogs?

Poochini.

Happiness is something that comes into our lives through doors we don't even remember leaving open.

ROSE WILDER LANE

It is pleasing to God
whenever you rejoice or laugh from
the bottom of your heart.

MARTIN LUTHER

A young child walked up to her mother and stared at her hair. As her mother scrubbed the dishes, the girl cleared her throat and asked, "Why do you have some gray hairs?"

The mother paused and looked at her daughter. "Every time you disobey, I get a strand of gray hair."

The mother returned to her task of washing dishes. The little girl stood there, thinking. She cleared her throat again.

"Mom?" she said.

"Yes?" her mother answered.

"Why is Grandma's hair all gray?"

Laughter is the sensation of feeling good all over and showing it principally in one place.

JOSH BILLINGS

Laughter is the shock absorber that eases the blows of life.

UNKNOWN

A cheerful look brings joy to the heart.

It is of immense importance to
learn to laugh at ourselves.

KATHERINE MANSFIELD

Always laugh when you can.
It's cheap medicine.

LORD BYRON

A reporter interviewed a 103-year-old woman: "And what is the best thing about being 103?" the reporter asked.

The woman simply replied, "No peer pressure."

A father was teaching his son to admire the beauties of nature.

"Look, son," he exclaimed, "isn't that sunset a beautiful picture God has painted?"

"It sure is, Dad," responded the youngster enthusiastically. "Especially since God had to paint it with His left hand."

The father was baffled. "What do you mean, son? His left hand?"

"Well," answered the boy, "my Sunday school teacher said that Jesus was sitting on God's right hand."

Laughter is God's hand on the shoulder of a troubled world.

Unknown

Show me an owl with laryngitis, and I'll show you a bird that doesn't give a hoot.

One of life's mysteries is how a two-pound box of candy can make a person gain five pounds.

Intaxication: Euphoria at getting a tax refund, which lasts until you realize it was your money to start with.

Laughter is the shortest
distance between two people.

VICTOR BORGE

Laughter is the brush that sweeps
away the cobwebs of the heart.

MORT WALKER

You're never fully dressed
without a smile.

MARTIN CHARNIN

Knock, knock.

Who's there?

Thermos.

Thermos who?

Thermos be a doorbell here someplace.

Knock, knock.

Who's there?

Warrior.

Warrior who?

Warrior been? I've been knocking for hours!

If you can't make it better,
you can laugh at it.

ERMA BOMBECK

I try to take one day at a time,
but sometimes several days
attack me at once.

JENNIFER UNLIMITED

I used to eat a lot of natural foods until I learned that most people die of natural causes.

UNKNOWN

Don't worry about the world coming to an end today. It is already tomorrow in Australia.

CHARLES SCHULZ

The sense of humor is the oil of life's engine. Without it, the machinery creaks and groans. No lot is so hard, no aspect of things is so grim, but it relaxes before a hearty laugh.

George S. Merriam

A smile starts on the lips,
a grin spreads to the eyes,
a chuckle comes from the belly;
but a good laugh bursts forth
from the soul, overflows,
and bubbles all around.

CAROLYN BIRMINGHAM

A man was lying on the grass and looking up at the sky. As he watched the clouds drift by, he asked, "God, how long is a million years?"

God answered, "To Me, a million years is as a minute."

The man asked, "God, how much is a million dollars?"

God answered, "To Me, a million dollars is as a penny."

The man then asked, "God, can I have a penny?"

God answered, "In a minute."

To laugh a bit and joke a bit and grasp a friendly hand. . . To tell one's secrets, hopes, and fears and share a friendly smile; to have a friend and be a friend is what makes life worthwhile.

UNKNOWN

There is nothing better than to be happy and enjoy ourselves as long as we can.

ECCLESIASTES 3:12 NLT

Beep. Hello. You are talking to a machine that is capable of taking phone messages. But first let me say that my owners do not need siding, windows, a new long distance carrier, and their carpets are clean. They make donations to charities of their own choosing and do not need or want anything else. If you're still with me, leave your name and number, and they will get back to you.

If at first you don't succeed,
skydiving is definitely not for you.

Never marry a tennis player,
because to him love
means nothing.

Any child can tell you that
the sole purpose of a middle name
is so he can tell when he's
really in trouble.

A mother's bachelor son invited her over for a meal. He had just gotten two new dogs and wanted his mom to see them.

When she sat down at the table, she noticed that the dishes were the dirtiest that she had ever seen in her life. "Have these dishes ever been washed?" she asked, running her fingers over the grit and grime. "They're as clean as soap and water could get them," he answered. She felt a bit apprehensive but started eating anyway.

The food was really delicious, and she said so, despite the dirty dishes.

When dinner was over, her son took the dishes, put them on the floor, whistled, and yelled, "Here, Soap! Here, Water!"

What kind of food will you find in heaven?

Angel food cake.

A teacher asked the children in her Sunday school class, "If I sold my house and my car, had a big garage sale, and gave all my money to church, would I get to heaven?"

"NO!" the children all answered.

"If I cleaned the church every day, mowed the lawn, and kept everything neat and tidy, would I get to go to heaven?"

Again the answer was "NO!"

"Well," she continued, "then how can I get to heaven?"

In the back of the room, a five-year-old boy shouted, "You gotta be dead!"

Teacher: "Shirley, compose a sentence that begins with I."

Shirley: "I is—"

Teacher: "Never say, 'I is.' It's 'He is' or 'She is,' but 'I am.' Begin your sentence, 'I am. . .'"

Shirley: "I am the ninth letter of the alphabet."

A teacher had just discussed magnets with her class. A bit later, she said, "My name begins with M, and I pick things up. What am I?"

Niles thought for a moment and answered, "A mom!"

A smile is a powerful weapon;
you can even break ice with it.

UNKNOWN

A four-year-old boy was asked to pray before dinner. The family members bowed their heads. He began his prayer, thanking God for all his friends and family members. Then he began to thank God for the food. He gave thanks for the chicken, the mashed potatoes, the fruit salad, and even the milk. Then he paused, and everyone waited.

After a long silence, the little boy opened one eye, looked at his mother, and asked, "If I thank God for the broccoli, won't He know that I'm lying?"

Cleaning your house while your kids are still growing is like shoveling the walk before it stops snowing.

PHYLLIS DILLER

You've reached middle age when
all you exercise is caution.

UNKNOWN

Teamwork means never having
to take all the blame yourself.

UNKNOWN

A "pillar of the church" passed away and was on his way to heaven. When he got to the pearly gates, he met an angel. The angel asked him what God's name was.

"Oh, that's easy," the man replied. "His name is Andy."

"What makes you think his name is Andy?" the angel asked.

"Well, you see, at church we used to sing this song: 'Andy walks with me, Andy talks with me.'"

If swimming is so good for your figure,
how do you explain whales?

Beauty is in the eye of the beholder.
If those eyes are nearsighted, all the better.

Reintarnation: Coming back to life as a
hillbilly.

A man was driving past a farm and saw a three-legged chicken running alongside his car. Suddenly, the chicken picked up speed and disappeared around the bend. The driver pulled to the side of the road and called to the farmer, "I just saw a three-legged chicken!"

"Oh yes," said the farmer. "We have a bunch of 'em. We have three people in our family, and we all like drumsticks."

"Well, how do they taste?" asked the motorist.

"Dunno," said the farmer. "We can't catch any."

Did you hear about the delivery van loaded with thesauruses that crashed into a bus? Witnesses were shocked, astounded, surprised, taken aback, dumbfounded, thunderstruck, startled, caught unaware. . . .

But let the godly rejoice. Let them be glad in God's presence. Let them be filled with joy.

PSALM 68:3 NLT

A little time for laughter,
A little time to sing,
A little time to be with friends
Will cure most anything.

BONNIE JENSEN

Doctor: "How is the boy who swallowed the quarter?"

Nurse: "No change yet."

Lisa: "I've heard that a milk bath is good for the skin, so I'll need enough to fill the tub."

Grocery Store Associate: "Pasteurized?"

Lisa: "No, just up to my chin will do."

A nearsighted minister glanced at the note that Mrs. Edwards had sent to him by an usher.

The note read: "Phil Edwards having gone to sea, his wife desires the prayers of the congregation for his safety."

The minister failed to observe the punctuation, however, and surprised the congregation when he read aloud, "Phil Edwards, having gone to see his wife, desires the prayers of the congregation for his safety."

Humor is a spontaneous, wonderful bit of an outburst that just comes. It's unbridled, it's unplanned, it's full of surprises.

ERMA BOMBECK

Knock, knock.

Who's there?

Theodore.

Theodore who?

Theodore got slammed on my nose.

Knock, knock.

Who's there?

Dewey.

Dewey who?

Dewey have to keep telling these dumb jokes?

Cheerfulness brings sunshine to the soul and drives away the shadows of anxiety.

HANNAH WHITALL SMITH

Laugh, if you are wise.

LATIN PROVERB

What do you call a grizzly bear with no teeth?

A gummy bear.

Little Tony was in his uncle's wedding. As he came down the aisle during the ceremony, he carefully took two steps then stopped and turned to the crowd. When facing the congregation he put his hands up like claws and roared loudly. So it went, step, step, turn, roar, step, step, turn, roar, all the way down the aisle.

As you can imagine, the congregation was near tears from laughing. By the time little Tony reached the altar, he was near tears, too. When later asked what he was doing, the boy sniffed and said, "I was being the Ring Bear."

If God wanted me to touch my toes,
He would have put them on my knees.

Unknown

The human body was wisely designed—
we can neither pat our own backs
nor kick ourselves too easily.

Unknown

The Ten Commandments were the subject of Miss Dixie's Sunday school lesson for five- and six-year-olds. After explaining "Honor thy father and thy mother," Miss Dixie asked, "Is there a commandment that teaches us how to treat our brothers and sisters?"

Without missing a beat, little Cindy answered, "Thou shalt not kill."

Attending a wedding for the first time, a little girl whispered to her mother, "Why is the bride dressed in white?"

"Because white is the color of happiness," her mother explained, "and today is the happiest day in her life."

The child thought for a moment and then asked, "So why is the groom wearing black?"

Tell people that there are 400 billion stars and they'll believe you. Tell them a bench has wet paint and they'll have to touch it.

I love deadlines. Especially the whooshing sound they make as they go flying by.

Antique: An item your grandparents bought, your parents got rid of, and now you're buying again.

A woman and her five-year-old son were headed to McDonald's. On the way, they passed a car accident. As was their habit when seeing an accident, they prayed for whoever was involved.

After the mother prayed, she asked her son if he would, too. "Please, God," he prayed, "don't let those cars be blocking the entrance to McDonald's."

A cop pulls a woman over and says, "Let me see your driver's license, lady."

The woman replies, "I wish you people would get your act together. One day you take away my license, and the next day you ask me to show it."

Laughter is the sun that drives
winter from the face.

VICTOR HUGO

Those who bring sunshine
to the lives of others cannot keep
it from themselves.

J. M. BARRIE

All praise to God, the Father of our Lord Jesus Christ, who has blessed us with every spiritual blessing in the heavenly realms because we are united with Christ.

EPHESIANS 1:3 NLT

Sign posted in a school cafeteria:

SHOES ARE REQUIRED TO EAT IN THE CAFETERIA.

Handwritten underneath:

Socks can eat wherever they like.

Everyone is beautiful
when sharing laughter.

Unknown

Every now and then, it's delightful to
have the kind of laugh that makes your
stomach jiggle, that sends tears down
your face, and causes your eyes to
squint so it's impossible to see!

Bonnie Jensen

If baby pigs are called piglets, why aren't baby bulls called bullets and baby chickens chicklets?

My cat is so smart. He eats cheese, then waits at the mouse hole with baited breath.

Why did Mozart sell his chickens?
    They kept saying, "Bach, Bach, Bach."

Part of the secret of a success
in life is to eat what you like and let
the food fight it out inside.

MARK TWAIN

Bert and Ernie are two Christians who have lived very good and healthy lives. They die and arrive in heaven. Walking along one of the golden streets and marveling at all the paradise around them, Ernie turns to Bert and says, "Wow! I never knew heaven was going to be as good as this."

"Yeah," says Bert. "And just think, if we hadn't eaten all that oat bran, we could have gotten here ten years earlier."

What did the teddy bear say when he was offered dessert?

"No thanks, I'm stuffed."

What do you call an apple with a short temper?

A crab apple.

What did the mayonnaise say to the refrigerator?

"Close the door! I'm dressing."

Happiness is like jam.
You can't spread even a little
without getting some on yourself.

UNKNOWN

At a church dinner, there was a pile of apples on one end of a table with a sign that read, **Take Only One Apple, Please. God Is Watching.**

On the other end of the table was a pile of cookies where a youth had placed a sign saying, **Take All the Cookies You Want. God Is Watching the Apples.**

Any day is sunny that is
brightened by a smile.

UNKNOWN

An English professor wrote the words "A woman without her man is nothing" on the blackboard and directed the students to punctuate it correctly.

The men wrote: "A woman, without her man, is nothing."

The women wrote: "A woman: without her, man is nothing."

A real friend is not so much someone you feel free to be serious with as someone you feel free to be silly with.

SYDNEY J. HARRIS

Some Boy Scouts from the city were on a camping trip. The mosquitoes were so fierce, the boys had to hide under their blankets to avoid being bitten. Then one of the scouts saw some lightning bugs and said to his friend, "We might as well give up. They're coming after us with flashlights."

We don't stop laughing because we grow old; we grow old because we stop laughing.

MICHAEL PRITCHARD

A couple was enjoying a dinner party at the house of friends. Near the end of the meal, the wife slapped her husband's arm.

"That's the third time you've gone for dessert," she said. "The hostess must think you're an absolute pig."

"I doubt that," the husband said. "I've been telling her it's for you."

"Be happy! Yes, leap for joy! For a great reward awaits you in heaven."

LUKE 6:23 NLT

Laughter is not all "ho, ho, ho" and "ha, ha, ha." It's also a quiet inner warmth that spreads good vibes throughout the mind and body.

BIL KEANE

Each happiness of yesterday is a memory for tomorrow.

GEORGE WEBSTER DOUGLAS

A child was watching his mother delete e-mail messages from her in-box.

"This reminds me of the Lord's Prayer," the child said.

"What do you mean?" asked the mother.

"Oh, you know. That part that says, 'Deliver us from e-mail.' "

A Sunday school teacher asked her little students, as they were on the way to the church service, "And why should we be quiet in church?"

A little girl replied, "Because people are sleeping."

A smile is a curve that
sets everything straight.

PHYLLIS DILLER

Smiling is infectious,
You can catch it like the flu.
Someone smiled at me today,
And I started smiling, too.

UNKNOWN

Toward the end of a particularly trying round of golf, Troy was the picture of frustration. He'd hit too many fat shots. Finally he blurted out to his caddie, "I'd move heaven and earth to break a hundred on this course."

"Try heaven," replied the caddie. "You've already moved most of the earth."

God gives us our relatives—
thank God we can choose our friends.

ETHEL WATTS MUMFORD

Blessed are those who can laugh
at themselves, for they shall never
cease to be amused.

UNKNOWN

Humor makes our heavy
burdens light and smoothes the
rough spots in our pathways.

SAM ERVIN

One day a father was driving with his five-year-old daughter when he honked his car horn by mistake.

"I did that by accident," he said.

"I know that, Daddy," she replied.

"How did you know that?"

"Because you didn't holler at the other driver after you honked it."

Patient: "Doctor, sometimes when I wake up in the morning I think I'm Donald Duck; other times I think I'm Mickey Mouse."

Doctor: "How long have you had these Disney spells?"

Whenever you see food
beautifully arranged on a plate,
you know someone's fingers
have been all over it.

JULIA CHILD

The best way to cheer yourself up
is to try to cheer somebody else up.

MARK TWAIN

I try to avoid looking forward or backward,
and try to keep looking upward.

CHARLOTTE BRONTË

Play with life, laugh with life,
dance lightly with life, and smile
at the riddles of life, knowing
that life's only true lessons are writ
small in the margin.

JONATHAN LOCKWOOD HUIE

Teacher: "Felix, when is the boiling point reached?"
Felix: "Just after my father reads my report card."

"If you have ten pieces of bubble gum and you give away four, what do you have then?" the teacher asked.

"I have six pieces of gum and four new friends!" replied the student.

Two old friends met one day after many years. The one who had attended college was now quite successful. The other had not attended college and never had much ambition.

The successful one said, "How has everything been going with you?"

"Well, one day, I closed my eyes, opened my Bible, and pointed. When I opened my eyes, I read the word *oil*. So I invested in oil, and the wells flowed. Then another day I dropped my finger on another word and it was *gold*. So I invested in gold, and those mines really produced. Now I have millions of dollars."

The successful friend was so impressed that he ran home, grabbed his Bible, closed his eyes, flipped it open, and dropped his finger on a page. He opened his eyes and read the words *Chapter Eleven*.

Mirth is God's medicine.
Everybody ought to bathe in it.

HENRY WARD BEECHER

Good humor is a tonic for mind and body.
It is the best antidote for anxiety and
depression. It is a business asset.
It attracts and keeps friends. It lightens
human burdens. It is the direct route to
serenity and contentment.

GRENVILLE KLEISER

If you ever find happiness by hunting for it, you will find it, as the old woman did her lost spectacles—safe on her own nose all the time.

Josh Billings

"Rejoice that your names are written in heaven."

Luke 10:20 NIV

A smile confuses an
approaching frown.

UNKNOWN

Live by this credo: Have a little laugh at
life and look around you for happiness
instead of sadness. Laughter has always
brought me out of unhappy situations.

RED SKELTON

One Sunday morning Pastor Bob advised his congregation, "Next week I plan to preach about the sin of lying. In preparation for my message, I want you all to read Mark 17."

The following Sunday the reverend asked for a show of hands from those who had read Mark 17. Every hand went up. Pastor Bob smiled and announced, "Well, Mark has only sixteen chapters. I will now proceed with my sermon on the sin of lying."

The Bible says that joy comes in the morning. However, it does not mention which morning. And until it shows up, God expects us to keep searching for the joy in today.

BILL SEAVEY

Joy is a flower that blooms when you do.

UNKNOWN

If you smile when no one else is around,
you really mean it.

ANDY ROONEY

I've never seen a smiling face
that was not beautiful.

UNKNOWN

It was local election time, and one candidate was visiting all the houses in his area. At one house, a small boy answered the door.

"Tell me, young man," said the politician, "is your mommy in the Republican Party or the Democratic Party?"

"Neither," said the child. "She's in the bathroom."

Cheerfulness is what greases
the axles of the world.
Don't go through life creaking.

H. W. BYLES

Knock, knock.

   Who's there?

Annapolis.

   Annapolis who?

Annapolis red and round.

Knock, knock.

   Who's there?

Cereal.

   Cereal who?

Cereal pleasure to meet you.

Sense of humor, God's great gift,
causes spirits to uplift;
Helps to make our bodies mend,
lightens burdens, cheers a friend;
Tickles children, elders grin
at this warmth that glows within;
Surely in the great hereafter,
heaven must be full of laughter!

UNKNOWN

A man asked his wife, "What would you most like for your birthday?"

She said, "Oh, I'd love to be ten again."

He came up with a plan, and on the morning of her birthday, he took her to a theme park. They rode every ride in the park together.

Lunchtime soon came, so into McDonald's they went, where she was given a Big Mac with french fries and a milkshake. After lunch, he took her to a movie—complete with popcorn and soda.

At the end of the day, her husband leaned over and asked, "So, sweetheart, what was it like being ten again?"

She looked at him and said quietly, "Actually, I meant the dress size."

A laugh, to be joyous, must flow from a joyous heart, for without kindness, there can be no true joy.

THOMAS CARLYLE

A college student delivered a pizza to the Wilsons' house. Mr. Wilson asked him, "What is the usual tip?"

"Well," he replied, "this is my first trip here, but the other guys say if I get a dollar out of you, I'll be doing great."

"Is that so?" snorted Mr. Wilson. "Well, just to show them how wrong they are, I'll give you five dollars."

"Thanks!" replied the delivery guy. "I'll put this toward my textbooks."

"What are you studying?" asked Mr. Wilson.

The young man smiled and said, "Psychology."

The Reverend Billy Graham tells of a time early in his ministry when he arrived in a small town to preach a revival meeting. Wanting to mail a letter, he asked a young boy where the post office was. When the boy had told him, Dr. Graham thanked him and said, "If you'll come to the church this evening, you can hear me give directions on how to get to heaven."

"I don't think I'll be there," the boy replied. "You don't even know how to get to the post office."

Life is like a mirror—we get the best
results when we smile at it.

UNKNOWN

A sense of humor is needed armor.
Joy in one's heart and some laughter on
one's lips is a sign that the person down
deep has a pretty good grasp of life.

HUGH SIDEY

Every time you smile at someone,
it is an action of love, a gift to that person,
a beautiful thing.

MOTHER TERESA

It's not what you do once in a while,
it's what you do day in and day out that
makes the difference.

JENNY CRAIG

Worry weighs a person down;
an encouraging word cheers a person up.

PROVERBS 12:25 NLT

Life is a ticket to the greatest
show on earth.

MARTIN H. FISCHER

Joy is a net of love by which
you can catch souls. A joyful heart
is the inevitable result of a heart
burning with love.

MOTHER TERESA

A man hurried into the emergency room and asked an intern for a cure for the hiccups. The intern grabbed a cup of water and splashed it onto the man's face.

"What in the world did you do that for?" asked the man.

"Well, you don't have the hiccups anymore, do you?" asked the intern.

"No," he replied. "My wife is in the car—she has them."

There are souls in this world which have the
gift of finding joy everywhere and of leaving it
behind them when they go.

JEAN PAUL RICHTER

There are only two ways to live your life.
One is as though nothing is a miracle.
The other is as though everything is a miracle.

ALBERT EINSTEIN

Laughter gives us distance.
It allows us to step back from an event,
deal with it, and then move on.

BOB NEWHART

Happiness is a perfume you cannot
pour on others without getting a
few drops on yourself.

RALPH WALDO EMERSON

As Noah and his family were disembarking from the ark, they paused on a ridge to look back.

"We should have done something, Noah," his wife said. "That old hulk of an ark will sit there and be an eyesore on the landscape for years to come."

"Everything's taken care of," Noah assured her. "I left the two termites aboard."

Why was the rabbit so unhappy?

She was having a bad hare day.

What did one horse say to the other horse?

The pace is familiar, but I can't remember the mane.

Reverend Walker was scheduled to perform a special wedding ceremony immediately following the Sunday morning service. He planned to perform the rite before the entire congregation, but for the life of him, he could not remember the names of the two members whom he was to marry. He got around his dilemma this way: "Will those who want to get married now, please come stand before me?"

At once, six single ladies, four widows, and five single men stood, went to the aisle, and walked to the front.

The world always looks brighter
from behind a smile.

UNKNOWN

I believe that laughter is a language of God and that we can all live happily ever laughter.

YAKOV SMIRNOFF

It isn't our position but our disposition that makes us happy.

UNKNOWN

A police officer saw a woman sitting in her car with a tiger in the front seat next to her. The officer said, "It's against the law to have that tiger in your car. Take him to the zoo."

The next day the police officer saw the same woman in the same car with the same tiger. He said, "I told you yesterday to take that tiger to the zoo!"

The woman replied, "I did. He had such a good time, today we're going to the beach!"

A smile is the light in the window of your face that tells people you're at home.

PHILIP D. NOBLE

I think laughter may be a form of courage. As humans we sometimes stand tall and look into the sun and laugh, and I think we are never more brave than when we do that.

LINDA ELLERBEE

A nonagenarian was interviewed by a local newspaper reporter. "Do you have a lot of great-grandchildren?" the reporter asked.

"To tell the truth," confessed the matriarch, "I expect they're all pretty ordinary."

Family Friend: "How's your mom? As pretty as ever?"
Kid: "Yeah. It just takes her longer."

What did Cinderella say while she was waiting for her photos?

"Some day my prints will come."

There are two ways
of spreading light. . .
to be the candle, or the
mirror that reflects it.

EDITH WHARTON

Mr. Johnson was overweight, so his doctor put him on a diet. He said, "I want you to eat regularly for two days, then skip a day, and repeat this procedure for two weeks. The next time I see you, you should have lost at least five pounds."

When Mr. Johnson returned, he shocked the doctor by having dropped almost twenty-five pounds.

"That's incredible!" the doctor told him. "You did this just by following my instructions?"

The slimmed-down Mr. Johnson nodded. "I'll tell you though, I thought I was going to drop dead that third day."

"From hunger, you mean?"

"No," replied Mr. Johnson, "from skipping."

We were filled with laughter, and we sang for joy. And the other nations said, "What amazing things the LORD has done for them."

PSALM 126:2 NLT

A cloudy day is no match for
a sunny disposition.

WILLIAM ARTHUR WARD

A rather stingy man died and went to heaven. He was met at the front gate by St. Peter, who led him on a house tour down the golden streets. They passed mansion after beautiful mansion until they came to the end of the street and stopped in front of a tiny shack without gold paving in front.

"And here is where you will be living, sir," Peter announced.

"Me, live here?" the stingy man yelled. "How come?"

Peter replied, "I did the best I could with the money you sent us."

The only way to keep your
health is to eat what you don't want,
drink what you don't like,
and do what you'd rather not.

MARK TWAIN

Say what you will about the Ten
Commandments, you must always
come back to the pleasant fact that
there are only ten of them.

H. L. MENCKEN

Knock, knock.

Who's there?

Yachts.

Yachts who?

Yachts new, pussycat?

Knock, knock.

Who's there?

Izzy.

Izzy who?

Izzy come, Izzy go.

Everyone smiles in the same language.

UNKNOWN

If you would like to spoil the day for a grouch, give him a smile.

UNKNOWN

I have a tickle in my brain. And it keeps making the corners of my mouth point toward the heavens.

JEB DICKERSON

An elderly gentleman had serious hearing problems for a number of years. He went to the doctor and was fitted for a set of hearing aids that allowed the man to hear perfectly.

The elderly gentleman went back in a month to the doctor, and the doctor said, "Your hearing is perfect. Your family must be really pleased you can hear again."

The gentleman replied, "Oh, I haven't told my family yet. I just sit around and listen to their conversations. I've changed my will five times!"